SELLING BY OBJECTIVES:

The Handbook for More

Profitability in the 21st Century

2nd Edition

I0474163

by

Dr. Dave Hinkes

Dr. Daryl D. Green

FOREWORD by Dean Jack McCann

2nd Edition

For information on ordering in bulk, please contact:

PMLA
P.O. Box 32733
Knoxville, TN 37930-2733
(865)602-7858
advice@darylgreen.org
www.darylgreen.org

Dedication

I, Dave Hinkes, dedicate this book to Deb, my wife of 30 years, and Jenny, Missy, and Steve, our three kids, who have sacrificed so much and supported me 'to go ahead and do my thing'.

This book is also dedicated to the millions of entrepreneurs and business owners trying to survive in these uncertain times.

Table of Contents

Foreword

Prior to serving in my current role as the Dean of the School of Business at Lincoln Memorial University in Harrogate, TN, I have had the good fortune of serving as a business leader in manufacturing companies, small business ownership, customer service, and healthcare. Since joining academia, I have had the opportunity to get to know both authors as a supervisor, colleague, co-author, and friend. We each share a desire to educate future business leaders and to develop tools that can continuously improve business performance in real and genuine ways.

Both authors have contributed to my continuing education in business by their varied work experiences, academic experiences, and business research. They have both been in the "real-world" and know how to successfully market themselves and the companies they have worked for and consulted with.

This book is a practical guide for dealing with effective relationships with today's customer. This book emphasizes thinking about marketing in a new way. Focusing on customer relationships and building a customer-centered organization is relevant to today's business and makes it a practical takeaway for the reader. I am finding uses for this book in my role as a dean to better market my school and its programs.

The book, *Selling By Objectives: The Handbook for More Profitability in the 21st Century,* presents the topics of branding, quality, reliability, creativity, simplicity, flexibility, efficiency, and price in a clear and focused way. The authors spotlight these topics on building effective customer relationships, necessities in dealing with today's customers. The authors also use examples that depict real situations that further bring these topics to life.

This book is a practical guide to help the business leader, salesperson, or individual immediately and continuously improve performance. Using the practical skills and examples found in this book will make a positive difference in your business, career, and for you personally. The authors teach the readers to change the way they sell in ways that will immediately improve performance. If you want to increase your business sales, grow profits, or enhance your business career, continue reading and then recommend this book to your friends.

Dr. Jack McCann
Dean of the School of Business
Lincoln Memorial University
Harrogate, TN

Preface

Dr. Dave Hinkes

This idea came from the theory of Management by Objectives (MBO) in the 1950s and we have spun off from this much heralded concept to sales and marketing. If you can practice or role play your responses to these objectives originating from any source, then you will find that you will be closing more deals, building more wealth, and saving time and effort in the process. Albeit a book with a similar title was written by Alessandra, Cathcart, and Wexler in 1998, our book is different in the sense that it is all inclusive and self-contained; this makes the implementation for organizations simple to understand and execute. In fact, the beauty of this book is that it has universal readership in that everyone who desires to enhance personal and business relationships can do so more effectively by prioritizing this gem on your must read list.

Dr. Daryl D. Green

Like most Americans, I am worried about the direction of our country. People are losing their jobs. United States companies are finding it harder to compete abroad. Is there any wonder why some individuals want to give up? Dave asked me about doing a book project aimed at assisting businesses with strategic selling. I was hesitant at the time. I had a full-time engineering job, was teaching MBA students at Lincoln Memorial University, had a very active family of my own, and was working on an assortment of book development projects. Yet, when I look at the demise of American businesses, it was a project I could not pass up when I thought about the long term ramifications of a book about strategic selling. Dr. Dave Hinkes is one of the brightest experts in our field at providing organizations with selling skills that are both reasonable and practical for most businesses. I am happy to be a part of this partnership aimed at making businesses more competitive across the globe.

Selling by Objectives provides practical solutions that today's organizations can easily digest and implement even in an unstable economy. This book is important not for just sales people, but for anyone who is involved in selling goods and services and wants to be successful in the marketplace. Business owners, college students, professors, entrepreneurs, nonprofit organizations, and other sales organizations can benefit from this book. Every reader can encourage success by building a personal brand in addressing the seven objectives (quality, reliability, flexibility, simplicity, creativity, efficiency, and price) discussed in this book in order to satisfy customers' needs or wants.

Acknowledgement

Dr. Hinkes

I want to thank several people who were the driving force behind this book effort. First, are my wife, Deb, and kids – Jenny, Missy, and Steve. Second, are Sy and Maxine, my late and beloved parents. Third, is Daryl, my co-author, for his undying motivation to help others through his prolific publishing. And, finally, all the folks that have touched me in academia, corporate, and consulting spheres...I thank you for the ride!

Dr. Green

I wish to take this opportunity to first thank God for guiding my footsteps. I feel you need to surround yourself with a great support network, and I want to thank my wife, Estraletta, with being a true helpmate because I would not be successful without her. I want to also thank our immediate family—our children Mario, Sharlita, and Demetrius. You continue to supply me with plenty of love. I also want to thank my mothers—my mother-in-law, the late Mrs. Lucy Andrews, and my dear mother, Annette Green Elias; they have continued to keep me grounded by providing sound advice.

I would like to thank Lincoln Memorial University for allowing me to be a part of its dynamic School of Business. I am extremely grateful to Dr. Jack McCann, Dr. Michael Dillon, and Dr. Dan Graves for allowing me this great opportunity. I must also thank my Regent University family for giving me these vital academic tools to make a significant contribution to society.

We want to thank everyone who read, evaluated, and commented on our book. We want to especially thank Dr. Dahlia Cunningham for her support in this book development. We also appreciate the editing work of Dr. Natalie Whalen. It is because of the critical contributions and feedback of our supporters that this book will become a success.

INTRODUCTION

Jim Warehouse: *"Will, you can put your stuff in the office next door."*

Will Win: *"Jim, thanks for your help. I am excited about being a part of a great organization like yours."*

Sarah Nelson: *[walks into the room]: "Jim, why are you wasting Will's time, telling him your old war stories? We've heard them a thousand times. Why do you act like a storyteller on Sesame Street rather than the number one salesperson in our area? [smiles]*

Jim Warehouse: *[laughs]: "Storytelling is how you connect with customers and build relationships. Why...that reminds of the time I was working on a Navy ship...."*

Sarah Nelson: *[grabs Will and runs out the door]: "Jim, we've* *got to go and get Will's paperwork completed in HR. He'll have plenty of times for stories."*

The Nelson Ford Dealership is a small dealership in Knoxville, Tennessee. Sarah Nelson, a 60ish petite, blonde widower, is the owner of the dealership. Sarah has survived several economic crises due to her relationship selling. She has a small sales force of five mature salespeople. Against their wishes, Sarah hired Will Win, a 25 year old ex insurance agent. She liked his spunk and selling intuition. He had moved from Dallas, Texas to stay with his sick mother. Sarah had a gut feeling that Will's raw talent would help stimulate their sagging sales. Will, not wanting to ruffle feathers saw how they could make major improvements by changing processes and using technology. Yet, he felt he would first just try and fit into the culture. He was also waiting to get his insurance license in the state. Although he knew how to sell, he was unsure how long his learning curve would last.

Like Sarah Nelson attempting to navigate her small dealership under adverse conditions, many businesses are looking for better and more effective ways to manage their organizations. Talking about selling strategy would not make sense if we simply ignored today's market forces. We do not. Economic turbulence has overtaken the American way of life in so many ways. After weeks of massive declines across the global financial markets, businesses continue to be shell shocked. Should they attempt to expand their businesses or hold steady with an unpredictable market picture? In Europe and Asia, investors stand uncertain of their next moves. Even America was part of an economic casualty. On Friday, August 5, 2011, Standard & Poors downgraded the United State's AAA credit rating. The agency further warned that more downgrades could continue if Washington could not overcome the gridlock by both political parties on how to solve the nation's debt.[1] Petty political bickering has had a severe consequence on the economy. David Walker, the former chief of the Government Accounting Office, warned that America must get

---

[1] "How Bad Will it Get?" by Gary Straus, Richard Wolf, John Waggoner, & Matt Krantz

its financial house in order: "We've kicked the can down the road as far as we can. We are at the abyss."[2] Yet, political infighting will make this process difficult. For example, Congress was unable to reach an agreement to reauthorize the Federal Aviation Administration (FAA). As a result, 4,000 FAA employees were furloughed and over 200 aviation development projects were stopped. This resulted in thousands of construction workers being laid off and millions of government dollars being wasted. The number of bad economic things that happen when bad politics exist is endless. [3] With a weak job growth, many U.S. jobs continue to be shipped abroad. According to government estimates, an additional 1.2 million manufacturing jobs will disappear in America by 2018.[4] Something needs to change.

Is America in trouble? On a daily basis we are being required to answer that question subconsciously and openly by today's media pundits. It is a process you cannot win. If you answer 'no,' you are given a series of the latest occurrences in America to silence you and question your literacy and IQ since you

---

[2] "In America's next decade, change and challenges" by Rick Hampson
[3] "No ticket tax refund leaves fliers stuck with the bill" by Gary Stroller
[4] "In America's next decade, change and challenges" by Rick Hampson

answered 'no' to a question that should have been answered 'yes.' If you answered 'yes,' you are then bombarded with more questions about what can be done. In fact, recent economic reports have shown vulnerabilities in the United States economic engine including everything from manufacturing to consumer spending.[5] Even the latest positive economic news brings another sequence of gloom. For example, the job rate ticked down July 2011. However, American businesses are not creating enough jobs. With unemployment still hovering over 9%, most people did not feel there was much to be happy about related to the job outlook.

One of the smartest ways to retool the economy is by selling more products and services to domestic and international markets. Therefore, the art of selling becomes a critical competitive advantage to organizations that want to sustain profitability over the long-term. Selling is a common denominator for every business. No matter what business you are in, you must sell your product or services to customers. Yet, the concept of selling is related to creating value for customers. In creating values, businesses need to focus on two major themes:

---

[5] "Double-dip odds on the rise" by Scott Patterson

(a) Under-promise and Over-deliver which will provide repeat customers.

(b) Rapid Response which will focus attention on market forces, and careful attention to customer issues will go a long way in building trust and integrity.

Given these realities, selling is a people-oriented business that addresses the customer value proposition (See Figure 1). Therefore, an understanding of human behavior is pertinent and the ability to communicate well with various kinds of people is important. The field of selling can be very rewarding and exciting and for that reason, definite skills must be acquired in order for certain objectives to be met. Effective selling should focus mainly on information gathering, presentation, commitment and follow through.[6]

---

[6] *"Selling by Objectives"* by Tony Alessandra, Jim Cathcart, & Phillip Wexler

Figure 1: Customer Value Proposition

(An Attractive Offer – center of circle)

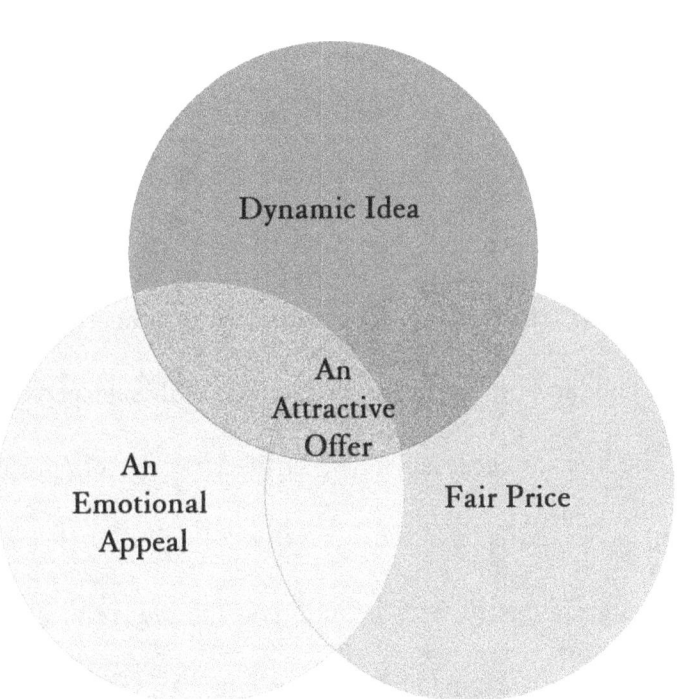

In the information gathering phase, everything must be thoroughly planned, studied and tested in order to prove that the products or services being considered are acceptable. Then the products or services may be presented or offered and the process can move into the phase of establishing relationships with clients and others.

Relationship skills can make or break important connections. Many such skills are discussed in the book, *Selling by Objectives*, written by Tony Alessandra, Jim Cathcart, and Phillip Wexler. The authors propose that successful salespersons will possess the virtues necessary to be at the top of one's profession: communication skills, the sensitivity and flexibility that enables one to create chemistry with people, and the ability to efficiently manage one's professional and personal life. Alessandra, Cathcart, and Wexler further believed that, basic to effective non-manipulative selling, is a sound understanding and the creative use of relationship skills which include tension management, relationship strategies, and characteristics of excellence.

Relationship selling and sales management are interconnected. Mark Johnston and Greg Marshall, authors of

Relationship Selling, note the importance of these connections: "The managers in the sales organization have taken time to think through the most efficient and effective way to manage the customer side of the business". Like any relationship, there is a degree of tension involved in selling due to relationship tension and the need for solutions. The tension may be positive or negative depending on how much exists or how it is handled. When a customer's tension level is identified, turning it into productive relationship-building energy is a technique that can be used by a successful professional salesperson. A professional salesperson will not only be able to identify and control tension levels, but also build up skills in relationship strategies. He will also be able to recognize potential customers' buying styles and be able to adjust his selling style to fit the styles of customers. The important skills of tension management and relationship strategies are always useful. Some suggested features helpful in achieving excellence as a salesperson are: knowledge, drive, taking risks, sensitivity, enthusiasm, creativity, honesty, being positive, flexibility and possessing a sense of humor.

Good communication is vital in building any customer relationship. In fact, communication represents power and a competitive advantage to salespersons who understand how to master this technique. Furthermore, Alessandra, Cathcart, and Wexler state that "selling is many things, but first and foremost it is a process of communication. It is a 'people' business in which you establish relationships, give and receive information, solve problems and build mutually beneficial associations with many people." Salespeople who are interested in excelling at what they do will focus on improving their communication skills even if they believe their skills are in tip top shape. Communication skills will involve both verbal and nonverbal communication. Sending and receiving messages must be clear for effective communication to be achieved. The verbal skills of listening, questioning, and giving feedback are all essential in selling. Nonverbal communication skills must also be acquired because body language, proxemics, and voice use and quality are important for business transactions on all fronts. Understanding communication will enhance your insight and put you in a position to be able to appreciate people's needs and motivation. It will also cause you to become a better communicator which will give you a better understanding and control of your personal and business lives.

Salespersons must also be competent and have a good set of sales management skills and abilities. To be a successful salesperson, you must treat your profession as a business and be your own sales manager. This requires developing the skills of proper territory management, effective prospecting, appropriate use of promotional strategies, and thorough preparation for sales calls with each potential client. Below are some key sales components:

- *Territory management* – the skill of managing a market segment or territory like a business.

- *Effective prospecting* – involves knowing how to keep the sales pipeline full by developing sources for prospects.

- *Promotional strategies* – cultivating them and setting up a system to qualify them.

- *Thorough preparation* – requires diligent research to identify what vital information is needed and where to find it; setting objectives and being fully prepared for all contingencies.

All the skills mentioned above will contribute to long-term, trusting business associations with your customers but they require enhancement by a variety of other skills that play an important role in professional sales. By using these skills in concert with each other, a salesperson can become a professional who develops long-lasting customer relationships based on trust and mutual understanding.

Selling by Objectives provides practical solutions that today's organizations can easily digest and implement even in an unstable economy. This book is important not for just sales people but for anyone who is involved in selling goods and services and wants to be successful in the market. Every reader can encourage success by addressing the critical selling factors. Guided by the principles of the relationship selling process, we have developed a seven step selling model for today's demanding customers (see Figure 2).

Figure 2: The New Relationship Selling Model for Today's Customer

"If your actions inspire others to dream more, learn more, do more and become more, you are a leader."

John Quincy Adams

1
Branding

Everyone in town went to the Nelson Dealership when they wanted to be treated like family and not hassled by salespeople. There was a story that one of the customers was promised a special order vehicle on a certain date. Unfortunately, the shipments got mixed up and the supplier said they could not meet that date. Rather than disappoint this high end client, Sarah called all around the country until she found exactly what the customer wanted. The story continued that she got Jim to drive up to Florida to get the car. She drove the car back and did not stop until she brought the car to the client's home all cleaned and polished.

Sarah understood that her personal brand of delivery was vital to her company's success.

In a world of let downs, a company's word is everything. When they fail to deliver, they are hurting their selling power. Yes, they are hurting their brand. Branding can be defined as a company's image in the marketplace. It is how customers view them in the sales market. Just seeing the Golden Arches will convince any child that he or she is close to McDonalds. That is how powerful an effective brand can be. A personal brand for individuals is just as important. Never dress inappropriately in a business setting or showcase a less flattering image on social networks such as MySpace, for future employers to view. The American Marketing Association (AMA) defines a brand as a "name, term, sign, symbol or design, or a combination of them intended to identify the goods and services of one seller or group of sellers and to differentiate them from those of other sellers".[7] Branding is about getting your prospective clients or customers to see you as the only person or business that provides a solution to

---

[7] "What is Branding and How Important is it to Your Marketing Strategy?" by Laura Lake

their problem. In fact, it all starts with proper identification, then image, then branding, then reputational influence.

Branding is the creation and development of your company's brand: The logo, images, slogans, ideas and other information connected to your company or product. Branding is part of the promotional decisions for organizations. In the context of the marketing mix, promotion represents the various aspects of marketing communication; that is, the communication of information about the product with the goal of generating a positive customer response. The marketing mix framework was particularly useful in the early days of the marketing concept when physical products represented a larger portion of the economy. Today, with marketing more integrated into organizations and with a wider variety of products and markets, some authors have attempted to extend its usefulness by proposing a fifth P, such as packaging, people, process, etc. Today, however, the marketing mix most commonly remains based on the 4Ps. Despite its limitations and perhaps because of its simplicity, the use of this framework remains strong and many marketing textbooks have been organized around it.[8] When we assume that the world actually *is* what we perceive, we get into all sorts of problems. Our minds lock down, and we form assumptions and opinions that are not based on any actual 'reality' so much as they are based upon our own ideas and perceptual biases. It does not take a scientific study for us to realize this. If we think about life, we will notice that all around us there are examples of misunderstanding, different opinions, and different tastes.[9] All of us have probably experienced times when our own opinions on a matter changed, or a taste that we did not prefer became desirable after we tried it a few times. Here we find the same implication — that our minds and ideas have a lot to do with how 'reality' is perceived.

Branding is what makes your company recognizable and unique. For the most effective branding, a memorable name and a ubiquitous slogan should be combined with an instantly recognizable and unique logo. A logo is the graphic or design by which your firm or product will come to be imagined by the customer. As in other elements of branding, simplicity can often be

---

[8] The Marketing Mix (The 4 Ps of Marketing) from Netmba.com
[9] "Perception Equals Reality" by Kentonwhitman.com

the best strategy. Your logo can be as straightforward as a simple geometric shape or, potentially, an elaborate design of a simple idea — such as a silhouette of a person or an object. In contrast to other elements of branding, your logo need not in itself be a clear representation of what your firm does, or what your product is. Its most important factor is being recognizable and unique. Therefore, a good brand will achieve the following objectives:

1. Deliver your message clearly.

2. Confirm your credibility.

3. Connect your targets or prospects emotionally.

4. Motivate your buyer or purchaser.

5. Make user loyalty concrete.

Once the logo has been chosen, it should be used regularly and consistently throughout your branding strategy, in order to represent your firm or product wherever possible. You should combine the elements of your branding — firm name, slogan and logo — on each piece of correspondence you make or advertising space you buy related to your product. This means that emails, letterheads, business cards, invoices, promotion and advertising, should bear the main elements of your branding. In doing this, your branding will be extended to the reaches of everything you and your products do, and will continue to spread the word of your growing success. One of the most famous examples from popular branding is Kentucky Fried Chicken's logo which is the 'Colonel Sanders' design — a smiling image of the face of the firm's founder. In itself, this iconic branding doesn't represent 'chicken,' or even food of any kind. But it is remembered in association with the name of the firm, meaning that as a whole package, its branding successfully keeps the firm lodged in its customers' memories.[10]

To succeed in branding, you must understand the needs and wants of your customers and prospects. You do this by integrating your brand strategies through your company at every point of public contact. Your brand resides within the hearts and minds of customers, clients, and prospects. It is the sum total of their experiences and perceptions, some of which you can influence, and some that you cannot. Furthermore, a strong brand is invaluable as the battle for customers intensifies day by day. It is important to

---

[10] "Branding" from http://articles.directorym.com/Branding-a520.html

spend time investing in researching, defining, and building your brand. After all, your brand is the source of a promise to your consumer. It is a foundational piece in your marketing communication and one you do not want to be without.

Gregory Berns, renowned expert, argues that branding is personal, involves a commitment, and requires dedication to a belief and the enthusiasm to work in a logical manner to gain acceptance of an idea. Put another way, branding is our way to put a little dent in the universe as it relates to technology and engineering education.[11] All we have to do is make the personal commitment to address the concept of branding. Then we must pursue branding with the enthusiasm of one who cannot wait for each day to dawn. When that happens, we will have put our little dent in the universe.

Clearly, the visual expression of your brand, your logo, is your identity and your signature. It makes a statement about who you are and what you stand for as well as how you are identified. Your brand identity is the focus of identity marketing and we combine that with our creativity and resources to bring you apparel and

---

[11] "Branding: Putting a Little Dent in the Universe!" from galegroup.com

merchandise that reflects your company. We specialize in the development, promotion and extension of corporate and brand trademarks through logo merchandise. We pride ourselves on integrating branded merchandise programs with marketing strategies. Let us help you leverage your brand identity and achieve your marketing goals. The concepts of corporate identity, communication, image, reputation, and branding have, at various times since the 1950s, captured the imagination of scholars and managers alike. The result has been new ways of conceptualizing organizations, new management functions and responsibilities, a new family of consultancy, and the emergence of new writing on corporations.[12] Furthermore, images and graphics are what many people remember most about your brand. Whether it is the elegant BMW logo or the simple Disney silhouette, logo design images often become the key recognition component of any company's marketing promotions. Over the long term, an elegant logo can bring in more business than an ad during the Super Bowl. The brand is all about how a business builds and packages its identity,

---

[12] "Revealing the Corporation: Perspectives on Identity, Image, Reputation, Corporate Branding, and Corporate-Level Marketing An Anthology" by John M. T. Balmer & Stephen A. Greyser

origins, and values and what it promises to deliver in order to emotionally connect with its employees so they in turn deliver what the business promises to its customers.[13] Therefore, a good image is a good selling point with customers. Your businesses reputation is the biggest determining factor in the long term success of any and all of your marketing efforts. Your reputation is recreated each day with each customer who encounters your business. In reality you are not limited to one business reputation, but many reputations that arise in the minds of customers who deal with you during your business activities. It is just as critical to remember that you have a reputation with people who have never done business with you but know of you from others.

There is a famous song by Joan Jett from days gone by called "Bad Reputation". Joan was a great musician of her time, but she also had a talent for marketing. She postured herself as the bad girl of the rock world, and the song "Bad Reputation" proved a hit. In the ever non-conformist scene of alternative rock, a woman proud of her bad reputation was very popular. She probably bent the truth

---

[13] "Segmenting Potential Employees According to Firms' Employer Attractiveness Dimensions in the Employer Branding Concept" by Lale Tüzüner

a little in the song when she sang "I don't give a --- about my bad reputation" as she obviously thought a good amount about her bad reputation; it was one of her best marketing advantages! She used that image to gain immortality. Unluckily for the majority of us, a bad reputation does not prove to be a useful marketing goal to develop our business. The only exceptions outside of musicians might be trial lawyers, repo men, or bail bondsmen who are known and valued for their dangerous air and fearsome reputation. For the rest of us it just does not work.

You have to be aware that everything you do, and everything your workers do, in the name of your business add to your reputation. You can attempt to correct things that might have put your business reputation in a bad light. In fact, remedying difficulties properly can be an opportunity in disguise. However, you will never change people's memory of what caused someone to take a low view of your company. Each experience you have with customers in your business has one of three results with your reputation at the core. Two of these results are not pleasant, the other one is terrific!

Experience #1 is when you have with a client, or potential client, where you do not do anything really wrong, but you also do not do anything to stand out from rivals. You may not think this is the worst outcome, but it comes close. You have managed to be, at best, average in the customer's view. The customer will either forget you in the future, or consider you a business that was just adequate last time.

Outcome #2 happens when you, or your worker, have errored massively enough to insure the patron is really mad at you. The worst has just happened for your business. Along with chasing away a patron, you have made certain you have lost those who learn of your business through that client. The negative potential is exponential. If you, as a business owner, are aware that you have permitted this to come to pass, then you deserve the problems to come. However, a great many times, the business owner knows nothing of what has occurred or if the problem was the employee's mistake, or out of their own interactions with the customer.

Do not believe that disgruntled clients will make time to let you know what occurred. Usually they just never set foot again in your business and no opportunity exists to fix it. If you uncover the problem, and then fail to make it right, then again you have earned the poor reputation it creates. However, if you take the time to go to every length to right the issue, you will have employed a fantastic opportunity in business to demonstrate to a patron that you care about their loyalty and will go the extra mile to demonstrate interest in making things right.

The 3rd outcome is sought by every savvy business owner in all interactions they have with clients. You aim to make the customers, and potential customers, believe that in addition to furnishing high-class services or materials, you are committed to how those products or services provide for a customer's desires. It is about establishing a trusting relationship with your clients so they know you will always focus on filling their needs. When you achieve this goal, you have formed a loyal customer whose value dwarfs any purchase they may make today.[14] Many experts working with all types of organizations offer various services giving advice on the use of social media as an essential part of research and reputation management. These tools work because

---

[14]"Your Business Reputation Is Built Daily" by Eric Menzies

they are essentially online versions of in-person networking. When you go to a conference or a gathering, you get to share what you do and what you enjoy with the people you meet. You get introduced by people you already know to new people you do not know yet. The same thing happens online. Because you are sharing your knowledge, expertise and personality, people can get to know you in more depth.[15]

On a deeper level, if we learn to observe our mind's activity, we can watch this process in action as our mind fixes on an apparent object or idea, locks down a perceptual 'snapshot,' and then skips away to whatever is next. Realizing this (or experiencing it if you are someone who enjoys observing your mind's activities) can create immense life changes. If you observe human conflict, almost all of it derives from disagreements of perception. When we believe that our perception is indicating a true reality, we can then consider the other person 'wrong', and that is a great excuse to yell at them, ignore them or hurt them. In the context of selling, what if you are a brand and you are trying to

---

[15] "Social Media: Essential for Research, Marketing and Branding. Detail" by Karen Blakeman & Scott Brown

engage your potential consumers? Unless these consumers are in your personal set of close friends, I would wager that your knowledge of how they perceive you can logically come from either assuming or asking. Assuming we assume, should we ultimately care most about whether sales are going up or going down? If more units are going through the cash register, we can happily report that public perception is up. But is it? There are many, many fabulous companies who deliver the most insightful and remarkable market research of samples of the population from which we scale the percentages to fit our market size. Decades of advertising expertise is piled onto the marketing strategy by exceptional and not so exceptional agencies who represent the brands and ensure that their product is presented to the market in the best way possible – earning the attention of consumers and providing ways for them to interact with the brand where possible.

However, once that has happened, the rest of the experience is in the hearts, minds and attitudes of the people. They are now the ones in control. We judge viewing figures on several tens of thousands of people and scale it to millions and millions...with a straight face. Every second of the day, somewhere in the world, a sample group is being asked what they think of a certain brand, product or service. How the people individually see the value of the product and the connection with the brand, is something that often makes painful reading – if it were to be written. We have to assume from sales, blogs, reviews, or scaled down groups that the perception is positive or negative. In this connected age where information exchanges over multiple platforms are quicker and easier than ever before, citizens have become journalists. We are all in control of the fate of brands now more than ever. If branding is done correctly, it will pay off over the long term.

"A man always has two reasons for the things he does—a good one and the real one."

JP Morgan

2
Quality

Ben State was notorious for finding a cheaper way of doing things. Working as a manager for a large discount store was an asset. However, sacrificing quality in exchange for less cost would get him in trouble with Sarah Nelson. Her clients knew Sarah as a business owner with an impeccable record of selling quality. As a favor, Sarah hired Ben because he was an in-law and was between jobs. Sarah provided her employees with an orientation about her expectations of quality. Ben had been hired as her procurement

49

specialist. He was in charge of buying parts. Jim had pointed out to Will that buying counterfeit parts overseas would not work at Nelson Ford Dealership. Will understood why it would be cheaper and most customers would not notice. Jim explained that Sarah would not allow it. During a routine walk around part of her operations, Sarah noticed two of her mechanics arguing about a part. Sarah walked over and found that one of the mechanics had been told to use this part that was not an original one. The other seasoned mechanic argued that he should not put this part into this car. Without saying another word, Sarah went into Ben's office and closed the door. One hour later, Ben could be found with his belongings leaving early. No one said a word about it. Ben was fired on the spot. Jim reminded Will that Sarah would not sacrifice the quality of her work. Ben was an example!

Many firms brag about their obsession with quality for their customers. Sadly, many customers learn through the firm's actions that the company is not really committed to quality. It then becomes a matter of all talk only. For high performing organizations, quality is an attribute that must compete with others in the marketplace. Tim Breithaupt, author of *10 Steps to Sales Success*, argues: "Technological changes, sales automation, deregulation, and the global economy have blurred many product distinctions, at the same time stimulating a highly competitive selling environment. Nowadays, product and price alone will not sustain a competitive edge."[16] Although there are many management techniques such as Six Sigma, Lean Manufacturing, and Total Quality Management initiatives to drive higher performance, most companies understand that quality is an inherent virtue that must become a mindset for employees and become deeply embedded in their corporate culture to be genuinely effective. John Dew, author of *Quality-Centered Strategic Planning*, places a high value in planning for quality: "Regardless

---

[16] "10 Steps to Sales Success" by Tim Breithaupt

of which standard one uses to measure the effectiveness of quality programs, be it the Baldrige Award, ISO 9000, or the Nuclear Quality Assurance-1 standard, quality must be planned into the fabric of the organization if it is to succeed."[17] Therefore, employees at all levels need to buy-in to the importance of quality if the organization hopes to sustain any marketable success.

Infusing quality into a product is not inexpensive. When there is a quality problem in a product that a customer finds, it is problematic for a company. For example, companies like Ford and Toyota would be hesitant to recall products due to the cost and negative publicity from it. As customers are engaged with a product or services, companies have little control over the outcomes.[18] In order to control the variability in quality, organizations must institute tight control over all manufacturing processes. This control includes educating all workers and conducting an effective quality control system upstream of the customer to prevent long-term quality control problems. Therefore,

---

[17] "Quality-Centered Strategic Planning" by John Dew

[18] "Quality Management" by Wall Street Journal (19 Sep 2007:12)

quality goes into a product or service even before the name of the company goes on it.

Some individuals identify with quality as 'the reduction of errors in an operation.' In fact, all manufacturing operations should seek the goal of zero defects due to the costly expense that errors bring. These errors lead to an assortment of problems including poor quality, rejects, recalls, rework, administration of warranties, market failures, and the harmed company reputation.[19] In order to achieve that, error proofing must be paramount. Error proofing enhances quality. This error proofing can be grouped in the following ways:

(a) physical - error proofing which involves installing components like fixtures or sensors to eliminate conditions that may lead to an error.

(b) operational - error proofing which involves making modifications or installing devices that reinforce the correct procedure sequence.

---

[19] "Quality Management" by Neil Fuller (*Supply Management*; April 15, 1999)

(c) <u>philosophical</u> - error proofing which involves identifying situations that cause defects and doing something about it - empowerment of the workforce, for example.[20]

Approaches to error proofing include prevention, which seeks to prevent errors from creating defects, and detection, which detects defects and immediately initiates corrective action to prevent multiple defects from occurring. Error proofing, as understood and practiced today, is an outgrowth of the quality movement, specifically, the zero defects initiative. Human error is natural. But sometimes, when errors can be traced back to the operator's interaction with the process, there is a tendency to blame the operator. We encourage the operator to try harder <u>not</u> to make mistakes, but the root cause of the error is usually failure on the part of people who design machinery, layouts, or operating procedures to account for the possibility of human errors or omissions. Error proofing can correct this situation. There are important facts to realize about human error. It is important to incorporate error proofing into the work environment.

---

[20] "Manufacturing Engineering" at http://www.sme.org

Understanding human limits is essential. Some people might find it easier to take shortcuts so that errors are not detected. In the short run, this may work. However, eventually shortcuts will hurt an organization in the long run. Researcher Neil Fuller rejects the paradigm of only looking at defects on the back end of the process. He argues that the concept of zero defects is no longer considered to be a sufficient tight criteria; the new trend is to move away from control and inspection toward early involvement of key players to institute quality principles.[21] Dave Thomas, founder of Wendy's said that the greatest lesson his grandmother taught him was, "Don't cut corners." At Wendy's, those words affect everything we do. "We don't cut corners with our hamburgers nor anything else for that matter. Our fresh, never frozen beef is always served hot off the grill. Our tomatoes are hand sliced and even our apples are hand-picked. You might wonder why we go through all this trouble. Well, our thought is: 'Real quality taste starts with real quality ingredients'."[22] Consequently, the new strategy is to focus

---

[21] "Quality Management" by Neil Fuller (*Supply Management*; April 15, 1999)

[22] "Don't cut corners" at Wendys.com (quality)

on building quality into the product at the design stage to avoid costly expenses such as rework or recall into the process. This new thinking requires involvement of both buyer and supply chain partners to make this strategy work.

"The key to successful leadership today is influence, not authority."

Kenneth Blanchard

3
Reliability

Will Win had gained Sarah's trust by his hard work and effective sales results. Will always listened to his customers and built a good relationship with him. It was this attitude that brought him a lot of referrals from past clients. On this day, Will was spending some time in Sarah's office learning about her company strategy.

Sarah Nelson: *Will, I've built my company by always considering my customers. Down the street, you will see many dealerships that focus on short term gains. Yes, they may be more profitable during some periods. However, my dealership has been profitable over* the years. Customers know that they can depend on me. It will work. Do you understand?

Will Win: *Yes, you are speaking about reliability. [remembering his operations management course, he spoke academically] Reliability is the notion that probability is a component part, equipment, or system that will satisfactorily* perform *its intended function.*

Sarah Nelson: *[smiles and pats him on the hand]: That's pretty good if you are teaching a college course. But---you'll lose most of my people. Reliability is about being dependable. Reliability is knowing that customers will have vehicles that work as intended. And, even if they do not work due to manufacturing error, it is my job as the customer advocate to make sure that it works as best as possible.*

Will Win: *[smiles back at her] I understand. We need to be dependable on all fronts. We will do this.*

[Sarah and Will walk off to the showroom].

Even in economic turbulence, opportunities will present themselves. Reliability is one of the key attributes that organizations need to take advantage of opportunities. Anthony Bloch, founder and owner of www.It'sTheRightWay.com, argues that incorporating trust, reliability, honesty and integrity into your business relationships is vital to being successful.[23] He further believes that our business relationships should be an extension of how we interact in our personal relationships. Your customers and business partners should receive the same standards that our friends and family receive in our personal relationships? There are four key elements of business relationships.

First, trust is central. We need to be able to trust business partners and vendors. If they are not living up to their obligations in being trustworthy, then perhaps there is a need to sever those relationships. We believe that the same expectation must be extended by business owners to their customers and business partners. Business relationships are a two way street. Both parties

---

[23] "Business Relationships Built on Trust, Reliability, Honesty and Integrity" by Anthony Bloch

should come out of the relationship having gained something. If only one party wins, then it's an unfair relationship.

Second, reliability means being there for the customer. It's our duty as businesspersons to offer reliable services to our customers. Always allow customer feedback and encourage visitors to your website to contact you if they encounter problems and try to resolve any issues that they may have.

Third, honesty relates to how sellers deal with their customers. We believe that people need to present the truth as they see it and be honest with their customers, stakeholders, and supply chain partners. If your partners and customers see you as an honest person, then they will be more likely to do more business with you. It's definitely in your best interest as a businessperson to conduct yourself in an honest manner.

Lastly, integrity speaks to the character of the organization. Integrity is a focus on a strong moral and ethical code. In our own personal lives, we see how a person's words and actions tell us about the character of that person. In fact, the personal in the selling rule is an ambassador to that organization. Therefore, businesses need to be careful about their sales representatives and the face of the company. Each person has a different code of morals and ethics. We believe that every businessperson needs to form their own code of conduct. Your business partners and customers will see you as a principled person who has a set of standards that can be trusted.[24] Organizations must always strive to meet the customer's needs. Our attention should be centered on our commitment to client satisfaction. Focus on communication, efficient project planning, and thorough execution. Companies should put their customer service policy in writing. Principles of customer service are all very well, but you need to put those principles into action with everything you do and say. There are certain "magic words" customers want to hear from you and your staff.

Neglecting any of these steps conveys the impression that you were interested in the person only until the sale was made. This leaves the buyer feeling deceived and used, and creates ill will and negative advertising for your company. Sincerely proving you care about your customers leads to recommendations and repeat

---

[24] "Business Relationships Built on Trust, Reliability, Honesty and Integrity" by Anthony Bloch

sales.[25] Reliability centers on being dependable. Customers can expect you to deliver on your promise. Most organizations are too busy focusing on the next sale instead of continuing to provide the needed service to existing customers. Therefore, being reliable and consistent play a vital role in competition when everything else is equal.

[25] "Ways to Show Your Customers They're Always Right" by Entreprenuer.com (Growing Your Business)

"You will always encounter folks who don't agree with what you want to do....Always hope for help but expect the contrary. It is the entrepreneur's dilemma."

Dr. Bruce Winston, author of *Be a Leader for God's Sake*

4
Creativity

Will Win wasn't satisfied until he found an idea to get more of the younger buyers for Nelson Ford Dealership. It was true that Sarah had built excellent relationships with families so that, in most cases, she would get young families to shop at her dealership. Yet, for young "twenty somethings," who wanted to be associated with their parent's automobiles? One of the more trendy dealerships had Starbucks shops in their offices and were always selling the most up-to-the-minute cars in the area. Yet, Will *understood that Sarah would not buy into ordering any of those vehicles that were all the rage and be stuck with them when the trend was over.*

One weekend, Will overheard a "twenty something" complain to his friend that this town was just too boring. What did college students have to do when they return home? Will knew this was a fact. On the other end of the spectrum, he knew several upstart bands that were looking to build a fan base over time. They would work inexpensively in order to sell their merchandise and have some regular income. Will shared his idea with several college students over the summer and got them to develop his concept to something that he could market to their generation.

Finally, it was "showtime". The parking lot was filled one Saturday night at Sarah's dealership. However, it was filled with a younger generation of customers. Initially, Sarah was reluctant that anything would happen. It did. Many younger people with families were buying from the dealership. Younger buyers were also spreading the word about going to this cool dealership on hot summer nights. Will's out-of-box thinking paid off for him that summer.

Creativity is the innovative search engine for today's organization. Robert Jacobs, Richard Chase, and Nichols Aquilano, authors of *Operations and Supply Management*, note the critical need for this attribute: "In our increasingly interconnected and interdependent global economy, the process of delivering supplies and finished goods from one place to another is accomplished by means of mind-boggling technological innovation, clever new applications of old ideas, seemingly magical mathematics, powerful software, and old-fashioned concrete, steel, and muscle."[26] "Entrepreneurs need to know that creative thinking isn't the only kind of thinking," says Berg, "because misplaced creativity can actually be harmful." For instance, after generating a lot of ideas, you need to be more analytical during the implementation phase. Staying in a creative mode may mean nothing ever gets done. Most people's formal education stresses analytical-style thinking over creativity. Yet, entrepreneurs who do not think effectively in both modes are missing a chance to build a competitive advantage.

---

[26] "Operations and Supply Management" by Robert Jacobs, Richard Chase, and Nichols Aquilano

Individuals need to implement creative ways of operations. Many individuals desire to showcase their ingenuity in an effort to create something like the works of Leonardo da Vinci.

Yet, creative thinking is not always easy. The pressures of time, cultural limitations, personal biases and even past successes can all combine to produce thinking that is rigid, overly analytical and uninspired.[27] Researchers have noted that culture is to the organization what personality is to the individual - a hidden yet unifying theme that provides meaning and direction.[28] Functional and hierarchical organizational subcultures emerge in response to both internal and external complexity and diversity. These divisions can create internal pockets of loosely coupled thought worlds.[29]

To harness the creative tensions inherent in modern organizations, it is necessary to build a cohesive series of stories, rather than a single tale. Each version must retain its distinctive view of the world, while combining its view with other versions. The challenge then shifts from attempting to merge completely

---

[27] "Good thinking: knock down the barriers to creativity - and discover a whole world of new ideas – small business management" by Mark Henricks
[28] "Recognizing Deep Structures in Organizations" by Martin Bowles
[29] "How Institutions Think" by Mary Douglas

incompatible thought worlds to promoting a chain of interactions among successively overlapping thought worlds. Different combinations of vertical and lateral thinking are necessary at different stages of an entrepreneurial process as it moves from rule breaking to rule keeping. Such shifts are not likely to occur within a given thought world. The interpretive dimensions that give rise to thought worlds are habits of the mind that tend to be fairly stable across time.[30] The creative process is still largely a black box, particularly when the process occurs within the mind of a single individual. Contradictory results of recent studies attempting to characterize creative individuals have been attributed to methodological problems of cracking that black box.[31] The quest seems to be for the right method to unlock the secret. This trend is discouraging, for it ignores a long history of research that strongly suggests that the creative mind is creative precisely because of inherent contradictions of character and personality.

---

[30] "How Institutions Think" by Mary Douglas

[31] "Use of Budner's Intolerance of Ambiguity Measure for Entrepreneurial Reports" by Marc Dollinger

Creativity Exercise (Da Vinci's Technique)

1. Think about a challenge you face at work.

2. Relax.

3. Allow your intuition to offer images, scenes, and symbols that represent your situation.

4. Provide a format for the challenge by drawing a boundary.

5. Draw as your mind wants to draw.

6. If one drawing does not seem enough, take another piece of paper and do another one, and another – as many as you need.

7. Examine your drawing.

8. Write down the first word that comes to mind for each image, symbol, scribble, line, or structure.

9. Combine all the words and write a paragraph.

10. Consider how what you wrote relates to your challenge[32].

The secret of creativity is not likely to be explained through rational, logical research. Inherent contradiction is not logical!

---

[32] "ThinkerToys" by Michael Michalko

Drawing on the psychological research of individual creativity and on theories of organizational innovation, this article has presented a framework for managing contradictions in corporate innovative processes. Contradiction is often what sparks creative breakthroughs in both individuals and in organizations. As managers of innovative processes, we need to encourage contradiction and conflict in our organizations. However, simply engaging in conflictive interactions will not necessarily culminate in collective creativity. Furthermore, the obstacles to creativity include experience, success, rigidity and conformity. To be creative you may have to ignore what you know, what has worked in the past, what feels comfortable and what everybody else is doing. Not surprisingly, then, most creativity tools and techniques are all about breaking rules. The best-known creativity tool is brainstorming. This can be done in a group or by a lone entrepreneur and requires only a sharp pencil, a piece of paper and a stream of consciousness. The idea is to rapidly generate new ideas without stopping to criticize or evaluate them. Therefore, today's organizations can use a variety of methods to infuse creativity.

In conclusion, studying creativity results suggest that creative processes require a balance of perspectives across both functional and hierarchical boundaries within organizations. However, creative activity is a process. It is motion that cannot be captured in a series of snapshots. Research must continue to expand the understanding of how the creative process unfolds in today's organizations. Further analysis of creativity will be able to effectively identify a set of components that both affect and are affected by this innovative system. By the application of creativity and innovation in organizations, the corporate knowledge will be forever embedded in its organizational culture to better foster creativity over the long-term.

"You must be the change you wish to see in the world."

Mohandas Gandhi

5
Flexibility

Jim was a man who lived by the rules. He expected anyone working with him to do the same. Several of his mechanics were new and younger. They were good workers. Yet, he noticed that some would come in an hour later on some days. However, they would make up any time without being asked. In fact, these men were very considerate about following the rules. Yet, Jim was a man who followed the rules. When Jim mentioned it to Sarah, she asked if he had talked with these young men about their tardiness. Jim didn't see the point. The men knew the rules. If they could not be to work on time, he would probably need to fire them and get someone who could be on time. Sarah understood Jim's rationale.

The dealership had plenty of work to be done and could not afford getting behind. However, this situation bothered her. One day she was in the breakroom talking and overheard some of these young men talking about taking their children to school due to the fact that their wives were working, also. Therefore, they would switch turns with taking the children to school. The situation was very clear now to Sarah. Yet, Jim was older than her and would not understand the situation. Therefore, Sarah did her research and found out how small businesses were assisting working families in balancing their time. She soon wrote a company policy about using flexible time to assist their workers. Jim thought it was a waste of time at first. However, he started seeing more of his employees getting things done faster. Flexibility worked.

Under the current economic crisis, business leaders who are rigid and unwilling to change will find it difficult to survive. Therefore, flexibility serves as a floatation device during business turbulence. Flexibility is very important for a business because changes must be made occasionally from initial plans to long-term strategies. Being able to change accordingly and always having the option to do so will make your business less vulnerable. In order to correct mistakes, errors, and inefficiencies swiftly, you must have the flexibility to do so. Flexibility means having the power, authority and system to change accordingly with ease. If you have the power and authority to change, then you are already quite flexible. However, true flexibility comes from the system of your business operation. The system of your business operation should be technologically easy and fast in responding to changes. Investing in technological tools and software that can make your business more flexible in making changes is a key factor in success. Upgrade your hardware and software to the latest and easiest setup for flexibility. Having the speed to react to changes is true flexibility in business. The flexibility to readjust, change and implement are important as scenarios and circumstances can change throughout time. Business is always uncertain, so flexibility is needed to accommodate it.[33]

[33] "Business Strategies" by David Kam

"Management is doing things right; leadership is doing the right things."

Peter F. Drucker

6
Simplicity

Anyone who knew Sarah understood she was a complex person. She did not mind being progressive in certain areas. She was one of the first owners in town to embrace technology by using a computer for her business. Yet, she was also an advocate for tradition even it was clear of a more progressive way. For example, Sarah would always send her customers a handwritten thank you note on any car purchase. Will understood the method; however, he attempted to convince Sarah that sending a personalized letter to the customer was a better option. Will would not give up on this initiative. Sarah finally stopped him from this weekly routine: "Will, I love your persistence. Many owners try to be too complicated in selling to customers. I like to keep it simple. It does not take me that much time to write these notes. But---you are missing an important part of selling. You got to understand your customers. Writing these 'thank you' notes help our customers who really appreciate the simple life. They are bombarded with junk mail daily. Do not make life too complicated or you will lose your customers." From that day forward, Will did not pursue convincing Sarah of this change. Will got it!

In a world of complexity and technology, simplicity becomes a challenge to customers and business executives who want to better connect with their market. There is a widespread philosophical presumption that simplicity is a theoretical virtue. This presumption that simpler theories are preferable appears in many guises. Often it remains implicit; sometimes it is invoked as a primitive, self-evident proposition; other times it is elevated to the status of a 'Principle' and labeled as such (for example, the 'Principle of Parsimony'). However, it is perhaps best known by the name 'Occam's (or Ockham's) Razor.' Yet, it is easy to see how customers could be lost. They are bombarded with multiple media messages. Simplicity is the answer. Simplicity can be defined as 'the state, quality, or an instance of being simple.'[34] Simplicity principles have been proposed in various forms by theologians, philosophers, and scientists, from ancient through medieval to modern times.[35]Cisco, which ranked No. 3 on the InformationWeek E-Business 100 list, started taking orders on its Website four years ago, and online commerce has steadily

---

[34] "Simplicity" defined at http://dictionary.reference.com/browse/simplicity.
[35] "Stanford Encyclopedia of Philosophy" at
http://plato.stanford.edu/entries/simplicity/

increased ever since. Nearly 85% of orders, an average of $37 million a day, are placed on the company's website. That is an increase of 71% over the number of web transactions Cisco customers placed a year ago.

But E-commerce to Cisco is not so much about making more money as it is about simplifying business processes and improving customer relationships.[36]

Why one simplifies something is as important as understanding where and how you make your living. Several reasons come to mind. For new law firms, such simplicity is generally rooted in a shared philosophy and similar practices or clients. For these firms, the economics and operating style of one practice versus another (within each firm) are not significant enough to warrant closer examination.[37] Citigroup is intent on simplifying its branding and will use the name Citi--in silver with a red arc above it--across all its businesses." Through a unified

[36] "Cisco Simplifies Business" by Brian Riggs
[37] "Even at its Simplest, a Not-So-Simple Business Practice" by James D. Cotterman

brand, we will leverage this symbol to represent our commitment to providing our clients with best-in-class advice, products and service," chairman and CEO Charles Prince said in a statement.[38] In the book, *Simplicity: The New Competitive Advantage in a World of More, Better, Faster*, Bill Jensen states that simplicity answers certain questions such as:

- What is your cost of confusion and the value of clarity?

- Are you using clarity to go faster, work smarter?

- Do you have a strategy for creating a simpler company?

- How will you continuously figure out what you don't know?

Jensen believes that you should either create less clutter or make more sense of it faster than the competition-and you win. [39] In the end he believes that simplicity is all about competing on clarity, being disciplined about how you make sense of things, being passionate about how you use people's time and attention.

---

[38] "Folding the Umbrella" by Katherine Burger

[39] "Simplicity: The New Competitive Advantage in a World of More, Better, Faster" by Bill Jensen

When everyone knows how to get what they need to make a decision, things will flow more efficiently. Therefore it is important to think of simplicity in these terms: Keeping it short and simple (KISS).

Some of the more positive attributes of a simple process include freedom from deceit and sincerity that all customers can appreciate. Despite all our advances in society, many people continue to make bad decisions. From million-dollar celebrities to business executives, there is a common denominator in the level of ineffective decision-making. Anthony Robbins, author of *Awakening the Giant Within*, attributes good decision-making as a key attribute to a happy life.[40] Robbins argues for the decisiveness of individuals making decisions: "I believe life is constantly testing us for our level of commitment, and life's greatest rewards are reserved for those who demonstrate a never-ending commitment to act until they achieve. This level of resolve can move mountains, but it must be constant and consistent. As simplistic as this may

---

[40] "Awakening the Giant Within" by Anthony Robbins

sound, it is still the common denominator separating those who live their dreams from those who live in regret."

Yet, too many times companies get caught up in their own internal complexities and convey these behaviors onto their customers. Yet, being too complex with customers can be very costly and carries many risks. Customers may not understand what a company is offering in terms of a product or service. In fact, customers may find it difficult to understand how your particular product or service addresses their immediate concern or need. If this happens, an organization is doomed because it puts a roadblock right in front of the customer. However, Jack Trout, author of *The Power of Simplicity: a Management Guide to Cutting through Nonsense and Doing Things Right*, offers the advantage of a simplistic strategy under the current climate: "Simplicity requires that you narrow the options and return to a single path....Complexity isn't to be admired. It's to be avoided."[41] Of course, many descriptions of the term simplicity are often not flattering, such as being called a 'Simple Simon'. In forging a

---

[41] "The Power of Simplicity: A Management Guide to Cutting Through Nonsense and Doing Things Right" by Jack Trout

single path….Complexity isn't to be admired. It's to be avoided."[41] Of course, many descriptions of the term simplicity are often not flattering, such as being called a 'Simple Simon.''. In forging a simple but effective approach to decision-making, the following strategies are suggested:

1. Define the problems or issues.

2. Conduct research on the matter.

3. Discuss problems or issues with respected individuals with similar circumstances.

4. Consider at least two alternatives.

5. Select the best decisions, based on your value system.

6. Monitor the solution and gather feedback.

7. Share the lessons learned at all levels of the organization.

Making the right decision is often a difficult process. However, it doesn't have to be complicated, especially if businesses are trying to sell to customers. Keeping things simple for your employees and customers should produce long–term benefits and greater sustainability over long periods of time.

---

[41] *The Power of Simplicity: A Management Guide to Cutting Through Nonsense and Doing Things Right* by Jack Trout

"Men cease to interest us when we find their limitations. The sin is limitations. As soon as you once come up to a man's limitations, it is all over with him."

Ralph Emerson

7
Efficiency

Foreign automobile manufacturers, such as Toyota and Honda, were beating American automobile manufacturers in all areas. All of the negativity went from the manufacturers to the local dealership. Sarah knew that many people in her own community were opting for foreign-built vehicles. At her staff meeting, Sarah warned her people that they needed to be more efficient in their operations. To her, it meant streamlining the

selling process to make it easier for customers. When she found that their loan department made customers wait too long in the office before they could get their cars, she made the loan department role play the process so they could see how the loan procedure was hurting sales. After the experience, the loan department rewrote its procedure. As a result, customers finished with the loan department and into their new cars 30 minutes sooner. Sarah realized it was the little things that would make a difference in competing with the foreign dealerships.

If organizations want to survive hyper-competitive environments, they must become more efficient and effective in their operations. Competition is fierce. Businesses try to build unique sets of competencies that are not easily duplicated by their competition. Robert Jacobs, Richard Chase, and Nichols Aquilano, authors of *Operations and Supply Management*, argue, "Competitive strategy is about being different. It means deliberately choosing a different set of activities to deliver a unique mix of values."[42] All businesses should seek to operate efficiently. In most cases, the process is very difficult. Being a success by becoming more efficient is another distinction. What do we mean by efficiency? It is where a business is operating at maximum output at minimum cost per unit of output. Efficiency is, therefore, a measure of how well the production or transformation process is performing. However, this is not always easy to assess. There are several ways to measure efficiency, which are:

Productivity

---

[42] "Operations and Supply Management" by Robert Jacobs, Richard Chase, and Nichols Aquilano

Productivity measures the relationship between input into the production process and the resultant output. The most commonly used measure is labor productivity, which is measured by output per worker. For example, assume a sofa manufacturer makes 100 sofas a month and employs 25 workers. The labor productivity is 4 sofas per person per month.

There are other measures of productivity such as:

- Output per hour/day/week
- Output per machine

Unit costs

Unit costs (also referred to as cost per unit) divide total costs by the number of units produced. A falling ratio would indicate that efficiency was improving.

Stock levels

A business will have set itself a target stock level of finished goods that it should achieve. This is calculated to satisfy the demand expected by the marketing department plans and based on what the production department thinks they can produce. Therefore, efficiency is particularly important for a growing business. In many markets, a business needs to be at least as efficient as its main competitors in order to be able to compete and survive in the long-term. A more efficient business will produce lower cost goods than competitors and may generate more profit possibly at lower prices. Increasing efficiency will also boost the capacity of a business, assuming there is no change in the number of inputs employed. Therefore, organizations that want to be competitive over the long run must improve their efficiency.

"If you don't understand that you work for your mislabeled 'subordinates,' then you know nothing of leadership. You know only tyranny."

– **Dee Hock**

8
Price

Ms. Claudia Weed, an elderly potential customer, came to the dealership looking for a particular car. Most people call her "Ms. Claudia." She explained that she was a widow on a fixed income. She gave him her price range. Will spent several days looking at various cars in her price range. Will worked intensively

with the loan department to find the right car for financing. He finally located what he thought was an appropriate deal for her and everything was ready. Ms. Claudia was coming by to pick her car. On her way, she ran into her sorority sisters who insisted that they would bring her. Will noticed that Ms. Claudia was acting strange when she arrived. She ignored him while the ladies looked at some of the most expensive cars. Ms. Claudia finally beckoned Will to look at one particular expensive car. Ms. Claudia informed him that she would get this car. Will politely mentioned that the staff had already cleaned up the car she had previously picked out. Ms. Claudia grew angry at Will's word and marched out with her sorority sisters to find a car at a different dealership. Sarah later explained that Ms. Claudia was high strung. She was embarrassed to get the used car she picked out in front of her peers. Sarah said she probably would have played along with Ms. Claudia's change of mind. From that time on, Will understood how factors other than price drive people like Ms. Claudia to buy.

Managing price is a key component of highly effective organizations. Price can be defined as "The amount of money charged for a product or service or the sum of the values that consumers exchange for the benefits of having or using the product or service." [43] Pricing is an important strategic issue because it is related to product positioning. Because there is a relationship between price and quantity demanded, it is important to understand the impact of pricing on sales by estimating the demand curve for the product. For existing products, experiments can be performed to adjust at prices above and below the current price in order to determine the price elasticity of demand. Inelastic demand indicates that price increases might be feasible. Furthermore, price is another component of the four Ps of the market mix, as explained below.[44] In general, marketing decisions generally fall into the following four controllable

---

[43] "The Four Ps of Google - Marketing Mix Price" at
http://articles.castelarhost.com/google_four_ps_marketing_mix_price.htm

[44] "The Amount of Money Charged For a Product or Service or the Sum of the Values that Consumers Exchange for the Benefits of Having or Using the Product or Service" by Gary Armstrong & Philip Kotler

categories which are product, price, place (distribution), and promotion.

The term "marketing mix" became popularized after Neil H. Borden published his 1964 article, *The Concept of the Marketing Mix*. Borden began using the term in his teaching in the late 1940s after James Culliton had described the marketing manager as a "mixer of ingredients." These four Ps are the parameters that the marketing manager can control, subject to the internal and external constraints of the marketing environment. The goal is to make decisions that center the four Ps on the customers in the target market in order to create perceived value and generate a positive response. While there is no single recipe to determine pricing, the following is a general sequence of steps that might be followed for developing the pricing of a new product:

(a) Develop a marketing strategy - perform marketing analysis, segmentation, targeting, and positioning.

(b) Make marketing mix decisions - define the product, distribution, and promotional tactics.

(c) Estimate the demand curve - understand how quantity demand varies with price.

(d) Calculate cost - include fixed and variable costs associated with the product.

(e) Understand environmental factors - evaluate likely competitor actions, understand legal constraints, etc.

(f) Set pricing objectives - for example: Profit maximization, revenue maximization, or price stabilization (status quo).

(g) Determine pricing - using information collected in the above steps, select a pricing   method, develop the pricing structure, and define discounts.

These steps are interrelated and are not necessarily performed in the above order. Nonetheless, the above list serves to present a starting framework.[45] It is extremely important for

---

[45] "Pricing Strategy" at
file:///C:/Users/Sunshine/Desktop/Selling%20by%20Objectives/Pricing%20Stra tegy.htm

marketers to remember that individuals in a market are highly receptive not only to the price of an item, but also to the value offered by the product. Successful companies such as Google take special consideration of the different parts involved in setting its prices. Items such as list prices, discounts, allowances, payment periods and credit terms are items that work together to set the price of a seller's merchandise. List price is one of the fundamental components of setting a price. The list price is defined as the, "Price normally quoted to potential buyers."[46] It is the basic prices offered to prospective consumers, yet in many instances, the price listed could increase or decrease as customers select options. Therefore, price decisions are critical. Some examples of pricing decisions to be made include:

- Pricing strategy (skim, penetration, etc.)
- Suggested retail price
- Volume discounts and wholesale pricing
- Cash and early payment discounts

---

[46] "Price Normally Quoted to Potential Buyers" by Louis E. Boone & David L. Kurtz

- Seasonal pricing

- Bundling

- Price flexibility

- Price discrimination

Additionally, pricing must take into account the competitive and legal environment in which your company operates. From a competitive standpoint, the firm must consider the implications of its pricing on the pricing decisions of competitors. For example, setting the price too low may risk a price war that may not be in the best interest of either side. Setting the price too high may attract a large number of competitors who want to share in the profits. From a legal standpoint, a firm is not free to price its products at any level it chooses. For example, there may be price controls that prohibit pricing a product too high. Pricing it too low may be considered predatory pricing or "dumping" in the case of international trade. Offering a different price for different consumers may violate laws against price discrimination. Also, collusion with competitors to fix prices at an agreed level is illegal in many countries. Lastly, a good pricing strategy needs to be in place for sustainable success and be continuously monitored. Before the product is developed, the marketing strategy is formulated, including target market selection and product positioning. Therefore, managers have the opportunity to design innovative pricing models that better meet the needs of both the firm and its customers. There usually is a tradeoff between product quality and price, so price is an important variable in positioning. Because of inherent tradeoffs between marketing mix elements, pricing will depend on other product, distribution, and promotion decisions.

Branding

Price

Quality

Efficiency

Effective
Relationships
with
Today's
Customers

Reliability

Simplicity

Creativity

Flexibility

"Nearly all men can stand adversity, but if you want to test a man's character, give him power." – **Abraham Lincoln**

CONCLUSION

After a year with the Nelson Ford Dealership, Will Win had become accustomed to an easy going environment. He had done very well with his sales quota and was much respected among his peers as a salesperson. From the very beginning, Sarah had conveyed the importance of relationship selling with all customers. Therefore, making a connection was important. Will always tried to build value for his customers. Little things meant a lot to Will's

customers. Will would send birthday cards, support school fund-raisers, and participate in the Chamber of Commerce events. Sarah awarded Will with the highest sales for the year and this meant a large bonus for him. Will used some of the bonus to buy his peers dinner. As time went by, Will became the co-partner of the Nelson Ford Dealership.

Will Win learned that selling was much more than pushing a product out of the door. After several years at the Nelson Ford Dealership, Will understood relationship selling in an intimate way. Perhaps, you don't have Sarah Nelson guiding you on the right path of effective selling. Yet, today's organizations cannot afford to not create the right kind of environment to nurture effective relationships with customers. During these times of rapid change and financial turmoil, businesses must find innovative ways to maintain corporate success through effective selling. Organizations that want to sustain success over the future need to retool their operations and build more intimate relationships with their customers. If salespeople do not understand market forces and relationship selling, they will be behind the times in the marketplace.

Relationship selling needs to be embraced at all levels of the organization. Buyers need to trust you. A salesperson needs to be an asset to the customer. Gaining influence is critical in achieving any substantial level in the market. When an individual has a platform, people listen. Therefore, salespeople become problem solvers with more influence on the customer. This influence allows an individual's opinion to be heard. Others start to accept your advice and ask for your recommendations. Increases in products and services soon will follow. Selling becomes a vital ingredient for sustaining profitability over the long-term. Consequently, businesses cannot forget creating value for customers. Value creation entails satisfying customers' needs or wants. *Selling by Objectives* provides a roadmap for today's organizations in an unstable economy. In this book, effective selling was broken down into several elements which were branding, quality, reliability, flexibility, simplicity, creativity, efficiency, and price. Optimizing these elements will provide organizations with a greater advantage and move them toward sustainable success in the future.

"It is not how long you live that counts but what you do in your life that is important. You've got to learn how to deal with the storms of life."

Rev. Richard Brown, Jr.

References

"10 Steps to Sales Success" by Tim Breithaupt

"Awakening the Giant Within" by Anthony Robbins

"Branding?" from http://articles.directorym.com/Branding-a520.html

"Branding: Putting a Little Dent in the Universe!" from http://0-find.galegroup.com.library.regent.edu/gtx/infomark.do?&contentSet=IAC-

"Business Relationships Built on Trust, Reliability, Honesty, and Integrity" by Anthony Bloch

"Business Strategies" by David Kam

"Changing Culture Generational Collision and Creativity" by Dane Leuenberger and Jodie Kluver

"Consensus, Diversity, and Learning in Organizations" by Marlene C. Fiol

"Determinant Attributes" from http://wiki.answers.com/Q/What_are_the_determinant_attributes

"Don't Cut Corners" at Wendys.com

"Double-dip odds on the rise" by Scott Patterson.

"The Four Ps of Google - Marketing Mix Price" from http://articles.castelarhost.com/google_four_ps_marketing_mix_price.htm

"Good Thinking: Knock Down the Barriers to Creativity - and Discover a Whole World of New Ideas - Small Business Management" by Mark Henricks

"How Institutions Think" by Mary Douglas

"How to Promote the Brand of You" by Paul Keegan.

"Identification of Determinant Attributes: A Comparison of Methods" by Mark I. Alpert

"In America's next decade, change and challenges" by Rick Hampson

"Manufacturing Engineering" from http://www.sme.org

"New Think: The Use of Lateral Thinking in the Generation of New Ideas" by Edward de Bono

"Operations and Supply Management" by Robert Jacobs, Richard Chase, and Nicholas Aquilano

"Our Business is Promoting Your Business" from http://www.logomojo.com/?kw_123cid=ME1031727

"Perception Equals Reality" by Kenton Whitman

"Price Normally Quoted to Potential Buyers" by Louis E. Boone and David L. Kurtz

"Pricing Strategy" from file:///C:/Users/Sunshine/Desktop/Selling%20by%20Objectives/Pricing%20Strategy.htm

"Production & Operations: Production Efficiency" from

http://tutor2u.net/business/gcse/production_efficiency_improvements.htm

"Quality Control Strategic Planning" by John Deer

"Quality Management" by Neil Fuller. (*Supply Management*; April 15, 1999)

"Quality Management" by Wall Street Journal (September19, 2007:12)

"Recognizing Deep Structures in Organizations" by Martin L. Bowles

"Relationship Selling" by Mark Johnston and Greg Marshall

"Revealing the Corporation: Perspectives on Identity, Image, Reputation, Corporate Branding, and Corporate-level Marketing An Anthology" by John N. Balmer and Stephen A. Greyser

"Segmenting Potential Employees According to Firms' Employer Attractiveness Dimensions in the Employer Branding Concept" by Lale Tüzüner

"Selective Perception: A Note on the Departmental Identification of Executives" by Dewitt Dearborn and Herbert Simon

"Selling by Objectives" by Tony Alessandra, Jim Cathcart, and Phillip Wexler

"Simplicity" defined from http://dictionary.reference.com/browse/simplicity

"Social Media: Essential for Research, Marketing and Branding" By Kareem Blakeman and Scott Brown

"The Amount of Money Charged for a Product or Service or the Sum of the Values that Consumers Exchange for the Benefits of Having or Using the Product or Service" by Gary Armstrong and Philip Kotler

The Marketing Mix (The Four Ps of Marketing) from Netmba.com

"The Power of Simplicity: A Management Guide to Cutting through Nonsense and Doing Things Right" by Jack Trout

"The Power of Simplicity: A Management Guide to Cutting through Nonsense and Doing Things Right" by Jack Trout

"Technology as an occasion for Structuring: Evidence from Observations of CT Scanners and the Social Order of Radiology Departments" by Stephen Barley

"The Act of Creation" by Arthur Koestler

"The Big Page of Branding & Corporate Identity Resources" from http://logoorange.com/branding-corporate-identity.php

"ThinkerToys: A handbook of Creative-thinking Techniques" by Michael Michalko

"Thought Worlds Colliding: The Role of Contradiction in Corporate Innovation Processes" by Marlene C. Fiol

"Use of Budner's Intolerance of Ambiguity Measure for Entrepreneurial Research" by Marc Dollinger

"Ways to Show Your Customers They're Always Right" by Entreprenuer.com

"What is Branding and How Important is It to Your Marketing Strategy?" by Laura Lake

"Your Business Reputation is Built Daily" by Eric Menzies

Glossary

Branding- The process of giving a product a distinctive identity by means of characteristic design, packaging, etc.

Creativity- The ability to transcend traditional ideas, rules, patterns, relationships, or the like, and to create meaningful new ideas, forms, methods, interpretations, etc.; originality, progressiveness, or imagination.

Effective Prospecting – Involvement of knowing how to keep the sales pipeline full by developing sources for prospects, using promotional strategies, cultivating them, and setting up a system to qualify them.

Efficiency- Accomplishment of or ability to accomplish a job with a minimum expenditure of time and effort

Ethics – The moral principles, values, or beliefs about what is "right" or "wrong."

Flexibility- The process related to being open to modifications or adaptations.

Price- The sum in money or goods for which anything is or may be bought or sold.

Quality- The process related to high grade, superiority or excellence.

Reliability – The ability to be relied on by someone or something for accuracy, honesty, or achievement.

Relationship Selling- The process related to the central goal of securing, building, and maintaining long-term relationships with profitable customers. Relationship selling works to add value through all possible means.

Simplicity- The concept related to freedom from complexity, intricacy, or division into parts.

Territory Management – The concept related to the skill of managing a market segment or territory like a business.

Value- The net bundle of benefits derived by the customer from the product you are selling.

Recommended Readings

Learn about information designed to enhancing marketing and selling efforts.

Business Management/Strategic Thinking

Microtrends by Mark Penn &Kinney Zalesne

The Portable MBA in Entrepreneurship by William Bygrave and Andrew Zacharakis

Thriving on Chaos by Tom Peters

Visionary Leadership by Burt Nanus

Visionary Sales Leadership by Ron McNamar

Global Market

Growing Your Business Globally by Robert Taft

Net Gain by John Hagell III

Net Worth by John Hagell III

Marketing Resources

Knock Your Socks Off by Jay Conrad Levinson

Guerrilla Marketing by Jay Conrad Levinson

Relationship Marketing by Regis McKenna

The Innovator's Dilemma by Clayton Christensen

Sales/Relationship Selling

10 Steps to Sales Success by Tim Breithaupt

Relationship Selling by Jim Cathcart

Relationship Selling by Mark Johnston & Greg Marshall

Sales Success Made Simple by Brian Tracy

Selling to Big Companies by Jill Konrath

About the Author

Dave Hinkes is a South Florida native who has been spent his whole life in the areas of office equipment, document management services outsourcing, mortgages, and sales/marketing training for companies like Xerox and IKON before going solo. He is affiliated with all of the professional sales and marketing associations, honor societies, and fraternities in which he holds all five of their professional certifications. He has been an adjunct professor at the University of Miami, Barry University, American InterContinental University (on ground, hybrid, and online deliverables), Florida Atlantic University, Miami Dade College, Northwood University, Nova Southeastern University, and Everglades/Keiser University teaching sales, sales management, marketing, management, negotiation, diversity, leadership/ethics, business research methods, operations management, real estate, mortgages, and strategy at all levels. He has conducted executive education and professional association seminars, consulted with mortgage companies, and has been a guest speaker for various groups.

He is currently an Associate Professor of Management and Marketing at Lincoln Memorial University in Harrogate, TN. He is published and cited in textbooks, websites, and academic and professional trade journals. His research interests are professional salesmanship, sales management, motivation, leadership performance, and cross-cultural values. He serves on the editorial review board for the Interdisciplinary Journal of Contemporary Research in Business (IJCRB). He is a recipient of a Teaching Excellence Award from the Accreditation Council for Business Schools and Programs (ACBSP). He is CEO of 'Hink, Inc.,' his own sales, marketing, management, and keynote speech consulting practice since 1991.

He holds a BA in Political Science from the University of Miami (Magna cum Laude), an MBA from Barry University, and dual DBA degrees in Management (11/02) and Marketing (4/09) from Nova Southeastern University. He is listed in the Who's Who in Professional Management, the National Association of Sales Professionals Registry of Who's Who, and the Metropolitan Registry of Who's Who Executives and Professionals.

He resides with his wife of 30 years, Debra, in Knoxville, Tennessee and has three adult 'kids' (Jennifer, Melissa, and Steven). He loves the theatre, basketball, football, bowling, table tennis, and golf.

His contact info is:

Dr. Dave Hinkes, DBA, DBA, CSE, CME, CPSP, PCM, SCPS
1239 Amber Meadows Circle
Knoxville, TN 37932
305.975.4354 Cell
HinkInc@aol.com Email
www.linkedin.com/in/davehinkes Social Networking
www.hinkinc.net My Company Website

About the Author

Dr. Daryl D. Green is a management strategist and a nationally recognized lecturer. Dr. Green loves developing intellectual properties to assist individuals with making better decisions. He is an adjunct professor at Lincoln Memorial University. He has also been a faculty member at Knoxville College. He has over 20 years of experience assisting organizations and individuals with making good decisions. Currently, Dr. Green is the author of several books and writes a syndicated online column on contemporary issues where over 3,000 online publishers and content providers around the globe have used his articles. His *FamilyVision* column is syndicated through the

Newspaper Publishers Association and reaches over 200 newspapers and more than 15 million readers across the country.

Additionally, Dr. Green has been noted and quoted by *USA Today, Ebony Magazine,* and the *Associated Press*. He has also been a freelance writer and guest columnist for various publications, including *Knoxville News Sentinel, Knoxville Enlightener, Discovery Magazine*, and the *IEEE Technology and Society Magazine*. He has also been a special assignment reporter for the *BIG Bulletin/Reporter*.

His professional experience includes management, engineering, research and development, marketing, and personal coaching. He received a B.S. in mechanical engineering and an MA in Organizational Management. Dr. Green received a doctoral degree in strategic leadership from Regent University. He has been a talk show host, a nationally recognized lecturer, nationally syndicated columnist, and personal advisor. Before his 30th birthday, he had already managed over 400 projects, estimated at $100 million dollars. These experiences place him in a unique position for understanding emerging trends. If you would like him to speak to your organization or would like more information about

his company services, please contact:

PMLA
P.O. Box 32733
Knoxville, TN 37930-2733
Phone: (865) 602-7858
Email: advice@darylgreen.org
Home page: www.darylgreen.org

Readers' Suggestions & Input

Our company is constantly updating our products so they are accurate and relevant. If you find missing information, we would like you to provide some suggestions, or if you have new information relevant to this discussion, please write, fax, or email us at:

PMLA
P.O. Box 32733
Knoxville, TN 37930-2733
Fax: (865) 602-7858
Email: pmla@att.net

Other Books by Dr. Green

Dr. Green continues to research and produce information that seeks to better society. Below is a synopsis of some of his other products:

A Call to Destiny: How to Create Effective Ways to Assist Black Boys in America provides a practical assessment of what happens to young black boys in America. It seeks to provide ways for parents, educators, and supporters to assist these boys in their positive development. Without any intervention, young black boys, regardless of their social class, will not survive in the 21st century. In this book, *A Call to Destiny*, you will (a) examine the severity of the problems facing young black boys, (b) learn new strategies to bring solutions to your child and the community at large, and (c) provide inspiration to continue the fight to save this generation of boys. (**Paperback:** 50 pages, **ISBN:** 978-1442181021)

Awakening the Talents Within is a powerful, step by step approach that individuals can use to solve problems and contribute to their overall success. This book is a wake-up call for the next generation of leaders. Dr. Green uses his charismatic style for today's hip hop culture, dealing with a wide range of issues from stopping procrastination to creating business ownership. The solutions contained in the book reflect over ten years of managing, consulting, and teaching in government, nonprofit, business, private and academic institutions. **(Paperback:** 136 pages, **ISBN:** 978-0595146130, **Hardcover:** 140 pages, **ISBN:** 978-0595745722)

Book Publishing for Professionals provides the secrets of gaining this useful power. Packed with proven insights and advice, this book provides simple, logical steps for professionals. It includes effective writing tools, best publishing options, and marketing strategies to make your book successful in the marketplace. It is geared toward the writer who wants to write a non-fiction book (biography, cookbook, self-help, Christian book, textbook, etc.). (**DVD**: 26 minutes, **ASIN**: B001FB4Z3G)

Breaking Organizational Ties provides practical strategies for employees attempting to cope in jobs or environments which they hate. While most managers are only concerned with the bottom-line, they leave their employees vulnerable to the casualties of competitive markets. This book will enable readers to (a) learn how to survive and even enjoy your time at work even in a hostile environment, (b) gain greater confidence in your ability to grow while in a downsizing organization, and (c) discover the insight to go beyond your limitations by breaking the barriers of your self-doubt. (**Paperback**: 124 pages, **ISBN**: 978-1450511315)

Impending Danger: The Federal Handbook for Rethinking Leadership in the 21st Century provides critical answers regarding how government leaders can reduce partisan bickering by changing the current leadership paradigm. With 40 years worth of experience in the public sector, Dr. Green and his co-author, Dr. Gary Roberts, know what they're talking about. They made sure that the book provides revelations and insights regarding political strife and the answers that can solve them. (**Hardcover:** 146 pages, **ISBN**: 978-1607971382)

Don't be an Old Fool: Common Sense & Gratitude is a collection of Dr. Green's syndicated columns through the years. The book offers practical strategies for individuals who desire to make better decisions in their lives by using sound, common sense approaches. With a new sense of direction, individuals will be able to re-energize themselves for the future. (**Paperback:** 134 pages, **ISBN:** 978-1466236530)

More Than a Conqueror: Achieving Personal Fulfillment in Government Service is a message about how to take positive steps in achieving your goals while in government service, although many individuals will be able to benefit from this book. In *More than a Conqueror*, you will (a) go beyond your self-imposed limitations by breaking the barrier of your self-doubt and (b) protect and cultivate your life in order to bring forth the best you can in your generation. (**Paperback:** 76 pages, **ISBN:** 978-0971400887)

My Cup Runneth Over: Setting Goals for Single Parents and Working Couples guides families in setting goals for themselves. Daryl and his wife have first-hand experience on this subject, both working full-time jobs, and raising three active children. This book uses a new management process called Meshing TM. The book is very different from most family books, by focusing more on practical solutions. Dr. Green has used his and his wife's experiences as managers from government, non-profit, and private business sectors to assist families in this country to do what we have done--take control of our family. Written in an informal, entertaining style, it provides information to families that give them HOPE. Creatively illustrated with graphics and charts, the book is also indexed for quick reference. It is essential reading for families in search of purpose.

Special Awards: January Book of the Month, The Larry Young Show 1998, Special Black History Award at Atkins Library, Featured on Heaven 600 (The Top Gospel Radio Station in the Country). **(Paperback:** 108 pages, **ISBN:** 978-1889745039, **Audiobook:** 978-1889745053, **Audio CD: ASIN:** B001VH787E)

Second Chance presents nonprofit organizations with a way to use operations management tools to make them more efficient and better equipped to assist their clients and constituents in meeting their needs. Dr. Green co-authored this book with one of his students. Through the eyes of student Noriko Chapman, readers will be taken on a magical journey of overcoming a difficult situation in operations management and life. **(Paperback:** 130 pages, **ISBN:** 978-1461146070)